The lost science in business administration

Prepared by
Taha Bayomy Mohamed
Founder of genetic economy science

Table of Content

The lost science in business administration.

Introduction

Chapter One: The characteristics that must be available in the company's employees, according to the type of its activity.

Chapter Two: The effect of general expenses, debit interest and credit interest on the company's results.

Chapter Three: Determination of the efficiency degree of the company's employees in managing the basic activity of the company

Chapter Four: The new approach for granting the bank credit.

Chapter Five: The principles that must be taken in times of crisis and economic depression.

Introduction

This book is unmatched in business administration books. This book enables any employee who works for these jobs (who works in the human resources department - works in the production department - works in the marketing department - works in the financial department - works as a general manager - an employee in the credit department - a shareholder or as the owner of the company) or the informed reader who is interested in business administration to control practically all the administrative elements of the company. After reading this book in limited hours (as we meant that the number of pages of this book are limited, but with unlimited science), then the reader will find himself like someone who took the highest certificates, which are comparable to the CFA and MBA certification, where:

In the first chapter: The reader will learn one of the tasks of the HR manager as follows:

The talents are different among people in the business field.

The difference in the economic efficiencies' degrees of the products from each other and based on them the type of activity of the company is determined.

How do we discover the talents of people in the field of business?

How do we discover the economic efficiencies degrees of the products?

The characteristics that must be available in the company's employees, according to the economic efficiency degree of its products (how to put the right employee in the right job).

Practical example.

In the second chapter: The reader will learn some of the financial manager's tasks as follows:

What is meant by general expenses, debit interest, and credit interest?

Who is responsible for managing general expenses, debit interest, and credit interest?

What is the importance of determining the extent of the effect of general expenses, debit interest, and credit interest on the company's results?

What are the equations that determine the effect of general expenses, debit interest, and credit interest on the company's results and how to treat them?

Practical example to find out how this effect is happening.

In the third chapter: The reader will learn some of the tasks of the financial manager and the general manager as well as the shareholders or the owners of the company as follows:

The reasons for knowing the efficiency degree of the company's employees in managing the basic activity of the company.

What is meant by managing the basic activity of the company?

What is meant by the efficiency degree of the company's employees in managing the basic activity of the company?

What are the reasons that lead to weak the efficiency degree of the company's employees in managing the basic activity of the company?

How do we measure the degree of efficiency of the company's employees in managing the basic activity of the company?

How do we deal with the weak efficiency degree of the company's employees in managing the basic activity of the company?

Why do the company prepare an estimated budget?

Practical example.

In the fourth chapter: The reader will learn some of the tasks of the bank credit employee, the financial manager, the general manager, and the owners of the company as follows:

What is meant by bank credit?

Elements of the bank credit.

Knowing the company's ability to repay the loan and its interest by using financial analysis.

The criticisms directed at financial analysis.

Knowing the company's ability to repay the loan and its interest by using the basic estimated budget and the credit budget.

Advantages of using the basic budget and credit budget in granting credit to companies.

Practical example.

In the fifth chapter: The reader will learn some of the tasks of the financial manager, the general manager, and the economic consultants as follows:

The types of influences that affect the company's activity.

The extent of the impact of those influences (positively or negatively) on the company's activity.

Identification of the four elements that affect the working capital turnover rate.

Determination of the economic elements related to the economic situation that the country is going through and their impact on the company's activity.

The principles to be considered when the sales cost value increases for the company to continue competing in the market.

The principles to be considered when the company gives discounts on the selling price to continue the company in its competing in the market.

Practical examples.

The author

The characteristics that must be available in the company's employees, according to the type of its activity.

In this chapter: The reader will learn one of the tasks of the HR manager as follows

The talents are different among people in the business field.

The difference in the economic efficiencies' degrees of the products from each other and based on them the type of activity of the company is determined.

How do we discover the talents of people in the field of business?

How do we discover the economic efficiencies degrees of the products?

The characteristics that must be met by the company's employees, according to the economic efficiency degree of its products (how to put the right employee in the right job).

Practical example

The talents of people differ from each other in the business field that they do in terms of

The ability of people to speed up decision-making (such as it is required that the dealer in the stock exchange is characterized by the speed of wise decision-making, while the manager of the real estate company is required to be careful in making his decision).

The ability of people to withstand working pressures (in our example, we find that the dealer in the stock exchange endures great pressures imposed on him by the nature of work in the stock exchange as a result of the frequent change in securities prices in a very short time, while this pressure is not present in the field of real estate companies).

The ability of people to negotiate (in our example, we find that the dealer in the stock exchange does not have the ability to negotiate because he buys or sells according to the prices that are displayed on the screen or he postpones his decision. As for real estate companies, there is a large area of negotiation with dealers with the company).

The ability of people to communicate with the employees of the company (in our example, the dealer that deals with the screen of stock exchange must be characterized by strictness in terms of the obligation of his employees to prove the operations that he completes on the screen with the speed of their completion. While the matter is completely different with the manager of the real estate company, who must be flexible with his employees and takes their advice according to their specialists)

The difference in the economic efficiencies' degrees of the products from each other and based on them the type of activity of the company is determined.

As the talents of the people differed. Also, the economic specifications of the products differ from each other and based on these economic specifications the type of activity of the company is determined. As each type of activity requires the availability of the specific talents of the people who carry out this activity in order to achieve the required success (this is what we explained in our previous example in terms of work requirements in securities companies that deal with the stock exchange and the requirements of work in real estate companies).

Here the following questions appear

What are the products?

What is the basis that made the economic specifications of the products differ from each other and thus the type of activity differs from one company to another?

The following is the answer to the previous questions:

The answer of the first question:

The product is the goods or services, whether this product is made by the company or bought from others, so this product represents the main activity for which the company was established with the aim of selling it to achieve profits for the company

The answer of the second question

The basis on which the economic specifications of the products differ from each other and thus the type of activity differs from one company to another.

This basis is summarized in the efficiency degree of the product, which is the capacity of one product unit and the extent of its contribution to cover administrative and debit expenses to achieve net profits equivalent to the company's capital, so this efficiency depends on three elements are following:

The cost of the product per one unit.

The selling price per one unit.

The quantity that is produced and sold from this product

The degrees of the efficiencies of the products are divided into two groups, namely:

The first group: It includes the efficiency degrees of products (excellent - very good - good).

The second group: It includes the efficiency degrees of products (acceptable - weak - very weak).

Where the efficiency degrees of the products for the first group (excellent - very good - good) are characterized by the following:

These products are very profitable if properly marketed.

These products can absorb the increase in the cost.

These products can grant discounts on the selling price and deal with customer facilities.

These products can deal with bank credit.

These products can give bonuses to motivate the workers.

Where the efficiency degrees of the products for the second group (acceptable - weak - very weak) are characterized by the following:

These products achieve profits when the working capital turnover rate is large (The quantity of units produced is large and there are markets that absorb this quantity).

These products are not able to absorb the increase in the cost (so caution is required).

These products do not allow giving discounts on the selling price, and they do not allow dealing with customer facilities.

These products do not allow dealing with bank credit.

These products allow giving rewards after achieving the estimated budget and not before achieving the estimated budget to motivate workers.

Every human resource manager should prepare a questionnaire form according to the characteristics of each of the two groups regarding the economic efficiency degrees of products. He can be creative in developing questions from questionnaire form.

The following is an example of such questions

Regarding production management:

Do you prefer to make a product with high-quality specifications or produce a very large number of the product?

What is the number of years of experience in relation to the company's activity?

Do you prefer to deal with the production staff team in the spirit of cooperation or the spirit of the leader?

Do you care about the details of the product cost or the quality specifications?

Do you prefer to work under pressure or not?

Do you prefer to take carefully your decision?

Do you prefer to have time for creativity?

Does the time help you to produce what is needed (mention the number of hours and minutes)?

Regarding marketing management:

Do you prefer to use the method of negotiation and persuasion in the marketing process or to spread and open new markets?

Do you care about showing the quality and specifications of the product or prefer to sell the largest quantity of the product?

Do you prefer to deal with the marketing staff team in the spirit cooperation of or the spirit of the leader?

How do you deal with the purchasing power that is available to you in the markets?

Do you prefer to use the price flexibility for products in the marketing process or prefer to adhere to the specified price for products?

Do you prefer to use the facilities and discounts method to promote products or prefer to adhere to the company's policies in granting the facilities and discounts?

Regarding financial management

The financial manager and his staff must be distinguished by the following:

They have a logical thought in order to link the cause and the effect.

They must be distinguished by patience, which enables them to continuously supervise and follow up.

They must be creative in making models that give the required results.

They must take responsibility in order to face the obstacles that occur to the company.

They must be able to communicate with all departments of the company.

Regarding the general manager:

Do the many pressures of work affect your emotional stability or not?

Do you prefer to take your decision slowly?

If you made your decision quickly, would it confuse you?

How many years of experience, you spent in the same company's activity?

Do you prefer to use financial rewards to encourage workers?

Do you pay attention to the precise details of financial spending (whether in the cost of the product or the general expenses)?

Do you prefer to deal with banks, or do you rely on what is available to you from the company's funds?

How do we discover the economic efficiencies degrees of the products?

In order to determine the economic efficiency degree of the products, we will use one of the mathematical equations of the geometric genetic economy theory, which is as following:

Measuring the economic efficiency degree of the company's product = (Sales value - (Sales cost value +General expenses) * 0.5) / Net profit

Where the economic efficiency degrees of the products are divided into:

First group: excellent - very good - good

Second group: acceptable - weak - very weak – losses.

The degrees of economic efficiency are determined according to the following

The case of the profit

In this case, the degrees of economic evaluation standards are integer and positive numbers or integer and positive numbers including fractions. The degrees of economic evaluation standard are divided into

From 1 to 2 degrees, it expresses an excellent degree of profit

From 2.01 to 4 degrees, it expresses a very good degree of profit

From 4.01 to 7 degrees, it expresses a good degree of profit

From 7.01 to 12 degrees, it expresses an acceptable degree of profit

From 12.01 up to 50 degrees, it expresses a weak degree of profit

From 50.01 up to infinity degree, it expresses a very weak degree of profit

The case of equality

In this case, the degree of the evaluation standard is equal to undefined value (infinity)

The case of losses

When revenue is greater than the average cost and less than the total cost)

In this case, the degrees of economic evaluation standard are integer and negative numbers or integer and negative numbers including fractions

The case of losses

When revenues are equal to the average total cost

In this case, the degree of economic evaluation standard is equal to zero

The case of losses

When revenue is less than the average cost

In this case, the degree of economic evaluation standard is only positive fraction numbers

The characteristics that must be met by the company's employees, according to the economic efficiency degree of its products (how to put the right employee in the right job).

The requirements for each economic efficiency degree of the product (the type of the activity) with the talents of the people required to practice this activity (whether in the production manager's job - the marketing manager's job - the financial manager's job - the general manager's job) according to the following

Firstly: The characteristics that must be available in the production manager, according to the economic efficiency degrees of the products that has achieved by the company

In the case that the economic efficiency degree of product is (Excellent - Very good - Good) The characteristics that must be available in the production manager as follows

The production manager must be creative in producing products of high quality.

The required experience for production is not as important as what is required to improve the quality of the product.

He deals with the production staff team in a spirit of cooperation.

He is able to show the specifications and quality required for marketing.

He does not need to work under pressure.

He takes his decision carefully for creativity.

He has more time for creativity

In the case that the economic efficiency degree of product is (Acceptable - Week - Very weak). The characteristics that must be available in the production manager as follows

The production manager must be able to produce a very large number of the product.

The required experience for production is very important.

He deals with the production staff team as a Leader.

He must be very careful about product costs.

He can work under a lot of pressure.

He takes his decision quickly in order to complete what required from him.

He has not a time in order to achieve the produced quantity.

Secondly: The characteristics that must be available in the marketing manager, according to the degree of the economic product efficiency that has achieved by the company

In the case that the economic efficiency degree of product is (Excellent - Very good - Good) The characteristics that must be available in the marketing manager as follows

The marketing manager must be able to use negotiating style and persuasion in the marketing process.

He must be able to show the quality and specifications of the product.

He must be able to deal with the marketing staff team with a spirit of cooperation.

He must be creative in dealing with available purchasing power in the market.

He must be able to use the product prices with high flexibility in the marketing process.

He must be able to use the facilities and discounts to promote products of the company.

In the case that the economic efficiency degree of product is (Acceptable - Week - Very weak). The characteristics that must be available in the marketing manager as follows

The marketing manager must be able to spread and open new markets.

He must be able to sell a greater amount of product.

He must be able to deal with the marketing staff team with the spirit of the leader.

He must be able to collect cash.

He must be able to adhere to specific pricing of the products that he sells.

He must be able to adhere to company policies in terms of facilities

Thirdly: The characteristics that must be available the in financial manager

The financial manager and his staff must be distinguished by the following:

They have a logical thought in order to link the cause and the effect.

They must be distinguished by patience, which enables them to continuously supervise and follow up.

They must be creative in making models that give the required results.

They must take responsibility in order to face the obstacles that occur to the company.

They must be able to communicate with all departments of the company.

Fourthly: The characteristics that must be available in the general manager, according to the degree of the economic product efficiency that has achieved by the company.

In the case that the economic efficiency degree of product is (Excellent - Very good - Good) The characteristics that must be available in the general manager as follows

The general manager does not work under a lot of pressure at work.

He must take the decisions slowly.

This activity does not require great experience.

He can use financial rewards in order to encourage the workers.

In the case that the economic efficiency degree of product is (Acceptable - Week - Very weak). The characteristics that must be available in the general manager as follows

The general manager must work under a lot of pressure at work.

He must make the decisions quickly.

He must have the considerable experience that is required for the activity.

He must be careful in spending.

In the previous steps, we explained how to put the right man in the appropriate job in order to achieve success for the company after knowing the requirements of the economic efficiency degree of the product and its relationship to the characteristics required in everyone who occupies a position in the production department, in the marketing management, the financial management, and the position of the general manager.

We will give this practical example in order to explain this subject, which is as following:

If you are a member of the Human Resources Committee in order to appoint a production manager and you have the following data:

The cost of the product unit is 600 EGP and the share of this product from the general expenses is 200 EGP and the selling price of the product unit is 1000 EGP and the characteristics of two people applying for this job were as following:

The first person

He cares about the specifications and quality of the product.

He spends on developing the product.

He prefers to deal with the production staff team in a spirit of cooperation.

He prefers to take his decision carefully and not work under pressure to reach a good product.

The second person

He interests with the volume of required production.

He is very careful about the cost of the product.

He prefers to deal with the production staff team as a leader.

He prefers to take his decision firmly and quickly and works under pressure to accomplish what is required

The question: Which of the two persons would you choose to fill this job in this company and why?

To answer this question, you must know the economic efficiency degree of this product and thus the specifications that characterize this product, as we compare these specifications with the personal characteristics of applicants for this job and thus, we choose the right person for the job

We will use one of the mathematical equations of the geometric genetic economics theory as follows:

First: Determination of the economic efficiency degree of product

Determination of the net profit = The value of sales - (The value of sales cost + The value of general expenses)

= 1000 - (600 + 200) = 200

Measuring the economic efficiency degree of the company's product = (The value of sales - (The value of sales cost +The value of general expenses) * 0.5) / Net profit

= (1000- (600 + 200) * 0.5)) / 200 = 3

Looking at the above economic efficiency degrees, we find that degree of 3 is equal to (very good)

Second: By referring to the economic efficiency degree of the products that is equal to very good, we find this product is characterized by the following:

This product is very profitable if properly marketed.

This product can absorb the increase in cost.

This product can grant discounts on the selling price and deal with customer facilities.

This product can deal with bank credit.

This product can give rewards to motivate the workers.

Third: By referring to the table of characteristics required in the production manager, according to the degree of the economic efficiency of the product, we find that the first person who is characterized by the following:

He cares about the specifications and quality of the product.

He spends on developing the product.

He prefers to deal with the production staff team in a spirit of cooperation.

He prefers to take his decision carefully and not work under pressure to reach a good product.

The first person is the right person for this job.

Another practical question that leaves its solution for the generous reader for practical benefit.

If you are a member of the Human Resources Committee in order to appoint a marketing manager and you have the following data:

The cost of the product unit is 800 EGP and the share of this product from the general expenses are150 EGP, and the selling price of the product unit is 1000 EGP and the characteristics of two people applying for this job were as follows

The first person

He has the ability to use the method of negotiation and persuasion in the marketing process.

He has the ability to show product quality and its specifications.

He prefers to deal with the marketing staff team in a spirit of cooperation.

He is creative in dealing with the purchasing power of consumers.

He prefers the facilities in the marketing process.

The second person

He has the ability to spread and open new markets to market the company's products.

He has the ability to sell the largest amount of production.

He is preferred to deal with the marketing staff team as a leader.

He has the ability to collect cash.

He adheres by the specified price and company policies

The question: Which of the two persons would you choose to fill this job in this company and why?

After you have made all the equations to know the economic efficiency degree of the product, as well as knowing the specifications of the product according to this economic efficiency degree and knowing the specifications that must be available in the marketing manager according to the degree of economic efficiency. If your answer was the second person, your answer is correct.

Summary of this chapter:

Through this chapter, we got to know one of the most important tasks of the Human Resources Manager, namely:

How to place the right employee in the right job.

In this chapter: The reader will learn some of the financial manager's tasks as follows:

What is meant by general expenses, debit interest, and credit interest?

Who is responsible for managing general expenses, debit interest, and credit interest?

What is the importance of determining the extent of the effect of general expenses, debit interest, and credit interest on the company's results?

What are the equations that determine the effect of general expenses, debit interest, and credit interest on the company's results and how to treat them?

A practical example to find out how this effect is happening.

General and administrative expenses mean: The expenses that are required for the completion of the company's activity and related to the working capital turnover other than production costs. The general and administrative expenses must be deducted from income statement in order to reach the net profits. The general and administrative expenses may negatively affect the results of the company's business

Debit interests mean: It is the cost that is deducted from the income statement and may negatively affect its net profits, which arise when the company resorts to borrow from others, such as banks, so the so-called debit interest is calculated on this borrowing

Credit interests mean: It is the revenue that the company obtains other than the revenue resulting from the basic activity of the company, as these revenues may positively affect the outcome of the business when it is included in the income statement of the company

Who is responsible for managing general expenses, debit interest, and credit interest?

The financial manager is responsible for managing the general expenses, debit interest, and credit interest, because one of the most important duties of the financial manager's job is the following:

Management of funds,

He aims to achieve a profit is equivalent to the resources available to the company (whether it is shareholders 'equity or capital of owners - or facilities obtained at a cost such as loans - or facilities obtained without cost, such as suppliers' facilities)

Follow-up production management in terms of:

Does the company have a system for controlling stores (whether raw materials store or ready-to-sale goods)?

Does the financial department have a special department for the actual and standard costs of the company's products, or not?

Does the company have the necessary liquidity for the working capital turnover, or not?

Does the financial department have an assistant ledger of suppliers to know the balances that need to be paid?

Does the financial department prepare production budgets for follow-up in order to verify the productivity of the production department?

Following up the Marketing Department in terms of:

Does the costs department perform the scientific pricing of the company's products?

Are there follow-up forms to know the time that it takes for the finished product to be sold?

Are there follow-up forms to know how long it takes the marketing department to collect the sales value?

Does the financial department have a sales analysis book to know the sales volume for each product and the periods in which it is sold?

Does the financial department have an assistant ledger of clients to know the balances that required to be collected?

Is there liquidity for the definition of the company's products?

Is there liquidity to provide the company's products in the right place and at the right time?

Does the financial department prepare marketing budgets for follow-up in order to verify the productivity of the marketing department (Marketing Director)?

Follow-up of general expenses

Is there a financial regulation that specifies who has the right to approve the exchange and the ways of spending?

How to determine the review before and after expenditure.

How to motivate the workers and employees in the company.

Is there an analysis book for expenses so that they are controlled in order to make the appropriate decision regarding them?

Is there a negative impact of general expenses on the company's results or not?

Follow up on the loan repayments and their debit interest.

Does the financial department recommend dealing with banks or does it prefer to increase its capital?

Is the debit interest affecting the production cost and marketing process as well as on the income statement result?

Does the financial department prepare a credit budget for debit interest?

Is there an analytical book for loan repayment and its interest?

Following up on the company's liquidity surpluses.

Does the company exploit the excess liquidity of the company in the company's activity or outside it?

What is the effect of the outside revenues on the company's results?

Following up the results of the accounting system.

Does the financial department audit the movement and balances of the treasury?

Does the financial department audit the movement and balances of the banks?

Does the financial department audit the asset values of the company?

What is the period during which the financial statements are extracted (income statement - balance sheet - list of capital owners' rights - cash flow list)?

What are the financial manager's recommendations as a result of his extrapolation of the financial statements that improve the company's business performance?

Managing and securing the company funds

Does the financial manager create the insurance documents for the company's assets and its liquidity?

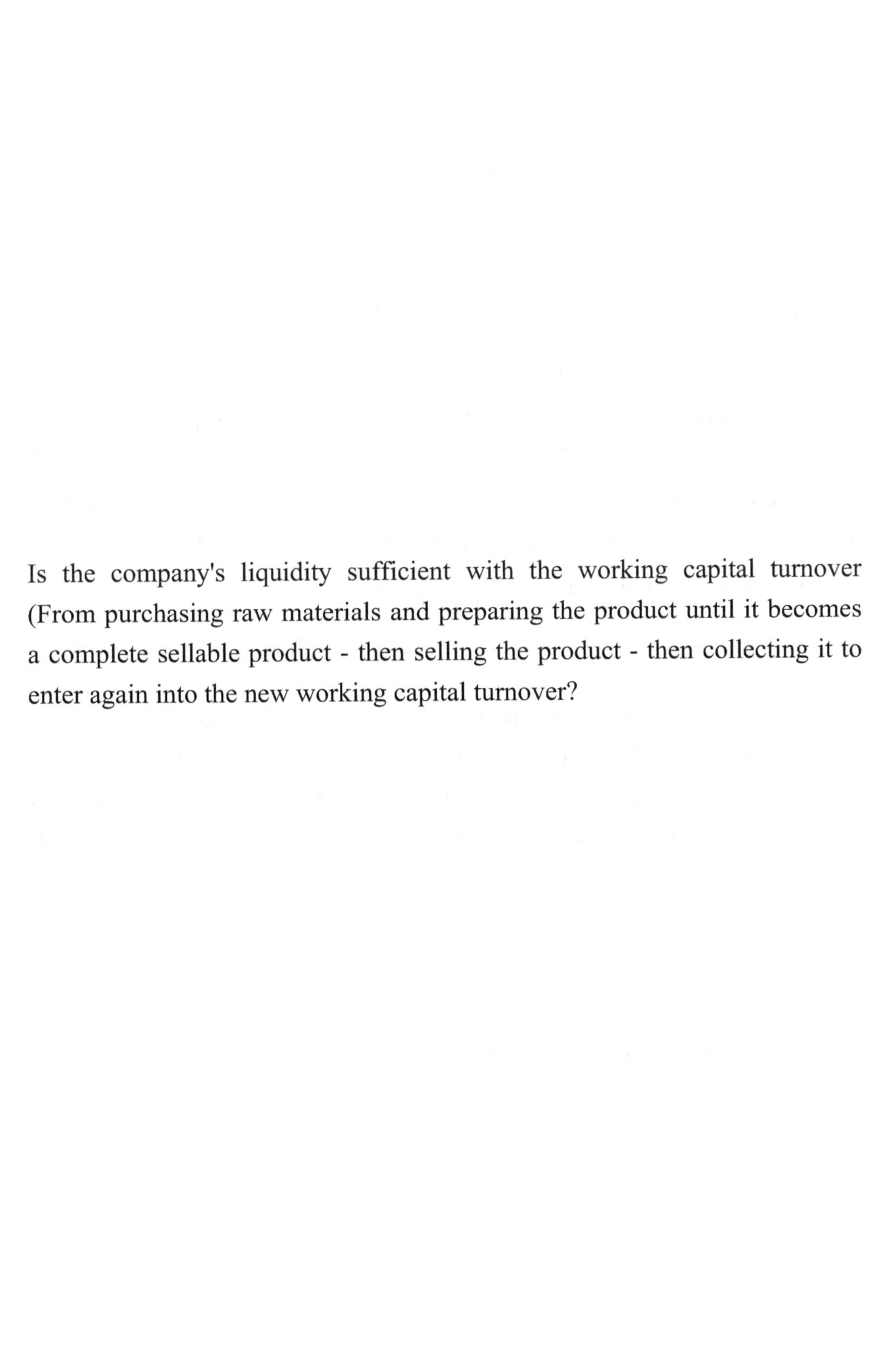

Is the company's liquidity sufficient with the working capital turnover (From purchasing raw materials and preparing the product until it becomes a complete sellable product - then selling the product - then collecting it to enter again into the new working capital turnover?

What is the importance of determining the extent of the effect of general expenses, debit interest, and credit interest on the company's results?

The importance of determining the extent of the effect of general expenses:

Here the company's administrators know practically whether there has been extravagant in the items of general and administrative expenses, including depreciation, or not. Or in other words, did the company preserve the profits that its products achieved, or were those profits lost as a result of this extravagance in general expenses?

The importance of determining the extent of the effect of the debt interest:

Here the company's administrators know practically the extent of the effect of the debt interest on the costs of the product. And is there possibility for the company's management to cover the value of the debit interest without affecting its results, or the debit interest has affected negatively the result that is achieved by the company?

The importance of determining the extent of the effect of the credit interest:

Here the company's administrators know practically the extent of the effect of the credit interest on improving the outcome of the income statement.

What are the equations that determine the effect of general expenses, debit interest, and credit interest on the company's results and how to treat them?

Firstly: Equations that determine the effect of general expenses on the company's results:

Here we will use some of the geometric genetic economics theory equations as follows:

First: Knowing the economic efficiency degree of the product without using general expenses, which is as following:

Measuring the economic efficiency degree of the product = (Sales Value - (Sales Cost Value) * 0.5) / Net Profit

Second: Knowing the economic efficiency degree of the product by using general expenses, which is as following:

Measuring the economic efficiency degree of product = (Sales Value - (Sales Cost Value + General Expenses Value) * 0.5)) / Net profit

Third: We compare the economic efficiency degree of the product by using general expenses with the economic efficiency degree of the product without using general expenses to find out whether there is a negative effect from general expenses or not according to the following.

The following table determines whether there is extravagance in general expenses or not

In case if the economic efficiency degree of the product without using general expenses is excellent

If the economic efficiency degree of the product by using general expenses became very good then, there is no negative effect of general expenses

Or the economic efficiency degree of the product by using general expenses became good - acceptable – weak – very weak – losses then, there is a negative effect of general expense

If the economic efficiency degree of the product by using general expenses became good then, there is no negative effect of general expenses

Or the economic efficiency degree of the product by using general expenses became - acceptable – weak – very weak – losses then, there is a negative effect of general expense

If the economic efficiency degree of the product by using general expenses became acceptable then, there is no negative effect of general expenses

Or the economic efficiency degree of the product by using general expenses became - weak – very weak – losses then, there is a negative effect of general expense

If the economic efficiency degree of the product by using general expenses became weak then, there is no negative effect of general expenses

Or the economic efficiency degree of the product by using general expenses became very weak – losses then, there is a negative effect of general expense

If the economic efficiency degree of the product by using general expenses became very weak then, there is no negative effect of general expenses

Or the economic efficiency degree of the product by using general expenses became losses then, there is a negative effect of general expense

In case if the economic efficiency degree of the product without using general expenses is very weak

If the economic efficiency degree of the product by using general expenses became very weak then, there is no negative effect of general expenses

Or the economic efficiency degree of the product by using general expenses became losses then, there is a negative effect of general expense

In case if the economic efficiency degree of the product without using general expenses is losses

If the economic efficiency degree of the product by using general expenses became losses then, there is a negative effect of general expense

Treating the negative effect of general expenses.

If the comparison is made according to the previous table, and it is found that there is a negative effect of the general expenses, the financial manager must make sure of the following two possibilities:

The first possibility: There is extravagance arising from items in general expenses, so the financial manager must specify these items and works to avoid them and apply the financial regulations that specify who has the right to approve the expenditure and aspects of expenditure and review the process before and after the expenditure in order not to repeat this extravagance.

The second possibility: when the extravagance appears in general expenses, not because of one of the items of general expenses, but because of the weak working capital turnover rate and its incompatibility with the available resources to the company. (For example, the company sold one deal in which it wins an amount of one thousand pounds and does not repeat it again during the year, while the annual general expenses amount is five thousand pounds) Here it appears what is called an extravagance in general expenses as a result of the weak of working capital turnover and the treatment for that is that the company repeats working capital turnover.

In order to explain this subject for us, we will give a practical example, which is as following:

If you are a financial manager and you have the following data:

The cost value of the product unit is 600 EGP and the share of this product from the general expenses is 300 EGP and the selling price of the product unit is 1000 EGP

The question is, is there extravagance in the general expenses of this company or not?

The answer:

To answer this question, we will use one of the mathematical equations of geometric genetic economy theory as follows:

First: Determination of the economic efficiency degree of the product without using general expenses, which is as following:

Determination of Net Profit = Sales Value - Sales Cost Value

= 1000 - 600 = 400

Measuring the economic efficiency degree of the company's product = (Sales Value - (Sales Cost Value) * 0.5) / Net Profit

= (1000 - (600) * 0.5) / 400 = 1.75

Second: Looking at the previous economic efficiency degrees table, we find that a degree of 1.75 is equal to excellent

Third: Determination of the economic efficiency degree of the product by using general expenses, which is as following:

Determination of Net Profit = Sales Value – (Sales Cost Value + General Expenses Value)

= 1000 - (600 + 300) = 100

Measuring the economic efficiency degree of the company's product = (Sales Value - (Sales Cost Value + General Expenses Value) * 0.5) / Net Profit

= (1000 - (600 + 300) * 0.5) / 100 = 5.5

Fourth: Looking at the previous economic efficiency degrees table, we find that a degree of 5.5 is equal to good

Fifth: you must look at the table of determining the extravagance or not, you will find that there is an extravagance in the general expenses, and this is due to the fact that the economic efficiency degree of the product without general expenses, which was excellent, but by using the general expenses the economic efficiency degree of the product became good without it passes a very good degree. Here, the financial manager must investigate the reasons for this extravagance, is it in one of the expense items or in the working capital turnover, and then treat the reasons that led to this extravagance.

After we know how to determine if there is a negative effect on the general expenses and how to treat it.

Here, this question appears: Do general expenses have a standard? (That is, the existence of maximum limits for the value of general expenses that should not be exceeded for each type of activity, and therefore this standard is considered a guide for the company in spending?)

The answer is yes, we will be able to know the standard general expenses through the selling price value of the product, cost value of the product, and the share of this product from the available uses for it (from current assets and fixed assets) to prepare a standard estimate budget that gives us the value of the standard general expenses of the company, which the company must not exceed, even by one pound, otherwise there is extravagance in general expenses. The following is an explanation of how to prepare the standard estimate budget.

Noticeable:

It is not necessary for the company to spend the full value of the standard general expenses, especially if the actual general expenses of the company are less than theirs. But the aim of knowing the value of the standard general expenses is a guide tool for administrators of the company.

Model of the standard budget preparation:

The aim of the model for the standard estimated budget preparation:
Rationalizing the available economic resources to the company and making the best use of them.
The standard estimated budget provides an opportunity to compare what was done with what was planned in that budget to find out the deviations and their causes and treat those deviations up to date.
Placing everyone in the company with his responsibilities entrusted to it.
The standard budget helps in making decisions regarding reward and punishment based on what has been achieved.
Determine who is responsible for not covering general and administrative expenses in the standard budget.
The standard estimated budget for new projects can be used as a reference in determining the value of general expenses that should not be exceeded to achieve the target of the project.

Inputs to the Budget Preparation model

The selling price of the unit (product).

Unit cost (product).
Total fixed and current assets.

Practical example

The following shows how the standard estimated budget model works if we have the following data:

The selling price of the unit (product)= 10 EGP
Unit cost = 8 EGP
Total fixed and current assets = 1,500,000 EGP
When the efficiency degree of the targeted budget is good (4.5) which is the start of the safety point that is sed in case of the current economic depression

Requirement: Preparing the standard budget.

The answer:

First: Calculating the degree of product efficiency for this company.

Calculation of gross profit = Selling price of the unit - Unit Cost = 10 - 8 = 2

Calculation of product efficiency degree = (Selling Price of the Unit - (Unit Cost * 0.5)) / Gross Profit

= (10 - (8 * 0.5)) / 2 = 3

Second: Determining the equivalent net profit to the available resources for this company by using one of the equations of geometric genetic economy theory

Estimated budget efficiency degree = (Total Assets - (Total Assets - Equivalent Net Profit) * 0.5) / Equivalent Net Profit

Assume that the equivalent net profit = B, and therefore the previous equation is as following:

4.5 = (1500000 - (1500000 - B) * 0.5) / B

4.5B = (1500000 - 750000 + 0.5B)

4B = 750,000

B = 187500

So equivalent net profit equals 187,500

Third: calculation of the sales value of the standard budget.

The table that determines the extravagance in general expenses are the following

In case if the economic efficiency degree of the product starts from 1 to 2

The degree of the efficiency standard, which indicates the maximum limits of general expenses that are permitted before the occurrence of extravagance, is degree 4

In case if the economic efficiency degree of the product starts from 2.01 to 4

The degree of the efficiency standard, which indicates the maximum limits of general expenses that are permitted before the occurrence of extravagance, is degree 7

In case if the economic efficiency degree of the product starts from 4.01 to 7

The degree of the efficiency standard, which indicates the maximum limits of general expenses that are permitted before the occurrence of extravagance, is degree 12

In case if the economic efficiency degree of the product starts from 7.01 to 12

The degree of the efficiency standard, which indicates the maximum limits of general expenses that are permitted before the occurrence of extravagance, is degree 50

In case if the economic efficiency degree of the product is greater than 12

The degree of the efficiency standard, which indicates the maximum limits of general expenses that are permitted before the occurrence of extravagance, is degree 1000

The product economic efficiency degree in this case is equal to 3 thus, the standard that indicates the maximum extent of general expenses before extravagance in this the case is 7 (see the previous table). Based on the above, we will use the standard (which equals 7) and the equivalent net profit (Which equals 187500) as data to obtain the sales cost value at the maximum limit of the standard of non-extravagance in general expenses as follows:

The sales cost value at the maximum limit of the standard of non-extravagance in general expenses = ((equivalent net profit * standard of non-extravagance in general expenses) - (equivalent net profit)) * 2

= ((187500 * 7) - (187500)) * 2

= (1312500 - 187500) * 2 = 2250000

The sales value of the estimated budget = the sales cost value at the maximum limit of the standard of non-extravagance in general expenses + equivalent net profit = 2250000 + 187500 = 2437500

Fourth: Calculation of the sales cost value for the standard estimated budget

After we reached the sales value of the standard budget (which is equal to 2437500), which resulted when using the degree of the standard of non-extravagance in general expenses (which was degree 7) based on the above, we will re-use the degree of economic efficiency of the product of this company (which was equal to 3) in order not to change from the type of activity of this company to find the sales cost value in the standard budget, so we will use the sales value (which equals 2437500) and the economic efficiency degree of this company's product (which was equal to 3) as data to obtain the sales cost value in the standard budget as follows.

Assume sales cost value = S.

Economic efficiency degree of the Product = (Sales Value - (S * 0.5)) / (Sales Value - S)

3 = (2437500 - (S * 0.5)) / (2437500 − S)

= (2437500 - 0.5S) = (2437500 - S) * 3

= (2437500 − 0.5 S) = 7312500 − 3 S

2.5 S = 4875000

S = 1950000

That is, the sales cost value for the standard estimated budget = 1950000 EGP

Fifth: Calculation of the gross profit of the standard estimated budget

The gross profit of the standard estimated budget = the sales value of estimated budget - the sales cost value of the estimated budget

= 2437500 - 1950000 = 487500

Sixth: Calculation of standard general expenses for this budget.

The value of the standard general expenses = gross profit value of the standard estimated budget - equivalent net profit value

= 487500 - 187500 = 300000

Seventh: From the above, we can prepare the standard estimated budget with a good degree as follows:

Sales Value =	2437500
Minus the sales cost value =	<u>1950000</u>
Gross profit =	487500
Minus general expenses =	<u>300,000</u>
Equivalent net profit =	187500

Note: The standard budget can be used in the preparation of feasibility studies, especially when it is difficult to determine the general expenses because the project is a new activity that will be practiced.

We will confirm from the achieved results.

The genetic economy does not leave any doubt about the results it extracts, so we find it is confirming the results as follows:

The standard estimated budget took into account the economic situation of the environment in which this company operates, as it used the 4.5 degree for the standard which indicates the beginning of the safety point and is used in the case of economic depression. How do we make sure of this? We know this by the degree of the efficiency of those responsible for managing the basic activity of the company as follows:

The degree of efficiency of those responsible for managing the basic activity = (Total Assets - (Total Assets - Equivalent Net Profit) * 0.5) / Equivalent Net Profit

= (1500000 - (1500000 - 187500) * 0.5) / 187500

= 4.5 (it is good degree)

It is the same standard that indicates the beginning of the safety point, which is used in the case of an economic depression, as we have applied in our case.

The standard estimated budget maintained the type of activity for this company, as follows:
The economic efficiency degree of the product before preparing the budget was as follows:

Calculation of Gross Profit = the selling price of unit - Unit Cost = 10 - 8 = 2

Calculation of the economic efficiency degree of the product = (The selling price of unit - (Unit Cost * 0.5)) / Gross Profit = (10 - (8 * 0.5)) / 2 = 3

After preparing the budget, the economic efficiency degree of the product continued as it is 3 degree in order to keep the type of activity and it is as following:

Calculation of Gross Profit = Value of Sales - Cost of Sales = 2437500 - 1950000 = 487500

Calculation of the economic efficiency degree of product = (Sales value - (Sales cost * 0.5)) / Gross profit = (2437500 - (1950000 * 0.5)) / 487500 = 3

The standard estimate budget has resolved the problem that occurs when the company cannot achieve the estimated budget. How we know who is responsible for not covering the general expenses, the marketing manager, or the general manager.

If the marketing manager does not achieve the sales value of the standard budget (in our case 2437500) then he is considered responsible for not achieving the budget and this is due to his inability to market the standard sales value.

If the achieved general expenses are greater than the standard general expenses (in our case 300,000) then the general manager is considered responsible for the non-implementation of the estimated budget, and this is due to the existence of extravagance in general expenses items. How do we make sure of this? This is what we will know in the following steps:

We can be sure of the case of non-extravagance when the general manager achieves general expenses up to an amount of 300,000, at the degree of standard 7, which we used to indicate that there is no extravagance in general expenses

Calculation of Net Profit = Sales value- (Sales cost + General expense)

= 2437500 - (1950000 + 300000) = 187500

Standard degree of general expenses= (Sales Value - (Sales Cost value + General Expenses) * 0.5) / Net Profit

= 2437500 - (1950000 + 300000) * 0.5 / 187500 = 7

It is the standard degree that indicates the maximum limits of general expenses that are allowed before extravagance occurs, as we have applied in our case.

The case of extravagance when the general manager achieves general expenses greater than the sum of 300,000, even if one pound.

Calculation of Net Profit = Sales value - (Sales cost value + General expense)

= 2437500 - (1950000 + 300001) = 187499

General Expense Standard degree= Sales value - (Sales cost value + General expense value) * 0.5 / Net Profit

= 2437500 - (1950000 + 300001) * 0.5 / 187499 = 7.000035

It should be noted on the standard degree of the general expenses that achieved which equals to7.000035 degree. It is more than the previous general expenses standard degree that was equal to 7 degree. Then we can say there is extravagance in general expenses.

From the above, we find that the standard estimated budget that is extracted by the mathematical equations of geometric genetic economy theory which has preserved all the following:

The efficiency degree of preparing the standard budget and consequently on the economic situation (which is 4.5 degree)
The economic efficiency degree of the product and thus the activity type of this company (which is 3 degree)
The standard degree of no extravagance (which is 7 degree)

This is the scientific miracle of genetic economy, as it was able for the first time to use the geometric theory outside of geometric science to reach the highest degrees of accuracy in the results.

Secondly: Equations that determine the effect of debit interest on the company's results:

We will use one of the mathematical equations of geometric genetic economy theory as follows:

First: Determination of the economic efficiency degree of the product without using debit interest, which is as following:

Determination of Net Profit = Sales Value – (Sales Cost Value+ General Expenses Value) =

Measuring the economic efficiency degree of the product = (Sales Value - (Sales Cost Value+ General Expenses Value) * 0.5) / Net Profit

Second: Determination of the efficiency degree of the product by using debit interest, which is as following:

Determination of Net Profit = Sales Value – (Sales Cost Value + General Expenses Value + Debit Interest Value) =

Measuring the economic efficiency degree of the product = (Sales Value - (Sales Cost Value + (General Expenses Value+ Debit Interest Value) * 0.5) / Net Profit

Third: We compare the economic efficiency degree of the product by using the debit interest with the economic efficiency degree of the product without using the debit interest to find out whether there is a negative effect on the debit interest or not according to the following table:

The following table determines whether there is a negative effect on debit interest or not.

In case if the economic efficiency degree of the product without using debit interest is excellent

If the economic efficiency degree of the product by using debit interest became excellent then, there is no negative effect of debit interest

Or the economic efficiency degree of the product by using debit interest became very good - good - acceptable – weak – very weak – losses then, there is a negative effect of debit interest

In case if the economic efficiency degree of the product without using debit interest is very good

If the economic efficiency degree of the product by using debit interest became very good then, there is no negative effect of debit interest

Or the economic efficiency degree of the product by using debit interest became – good - acceptable – weak – very weak – losses then, there is a negative effect of debit interest

In case if the economic efficiency degree of the product without using debit interest is good

If the economic efficiency degree of the product by using debit interest became good then, there is no negative effect of debit interest

Or the economic efficiency degree of the product by using debit interest became – acceptable - weak – very weak – losses then, there is a negative effect of debit interest

In case if the economic efficiency degree of the product without using debit interest is acceptable

If the economic efficiency degree of the product by using debit interest became acceptable then, there is no negative effect of debit interest

Or the economic efficiency degree of the product by using debit interest became weak very weak – losses then, there is a negative effect of debit interest

In case if the economic efficiency degree of the product without using debit interest is weak

If the economic efficiency degree of the product by using debit interest became weak then, there is no negative effect of debit interest

Or the economic efficiency degree of the product by using debit interest became very weak losses then, there is a negative effect of debit interest

In case if the economic efficiency degree of the product without using debit interest is very weak

If the economic efficiency degree of the product by using debit interest became very weak then, there is no negative effect of debit interest

Or the economic efficiency degree of the product by using debit interest became losses then, there is a negative effect of debit interest

In case if the economic efficiency degree of the product without using debit interest is losses

If the economic efficiency degree of the product by using debit interest became losses then, there is a negative effect of debit interest

Treating the negative effect of debit interest.

It is noticed that the table for determining the effect of the debit interest differs from the table for determining the extravagance of general expenses, this is because general expenses are among the compulsory items in the company's activity. As for the debit interest, its optional decision is due to the company's management.

If the comparison is made according to the previous table, and it is found that there is a negative effect from the debit interest, the financial manager must make sure of the following two possibilities:

The first possibility: If there is a negative effect of the debit interest, but the company can continue to pay the loan and its interest without the company facing insolvency in its financial liquidity, here the financial manager overlooks the effect of debit interest.

The second possibility: If there is a large negative effect of the debit interest, and the company cannot continue to pay the loan and its interest, as the company facing insolvency in its financial liquidity, Here, the financial manager must alert the top administration of the company to replace the loan and its interest by offering the alternative, which is to increase the capital.

In order to explain this subject for us, we will give this practical example, which is as following:

If you are a financial manager and you have the following data:

The cost value of the product unit is 600 EGP, and the share of the product from the general expenses is 100 EGP, the product's share of the debit interest is 200 EGP, and the sale price value of the product unit is 1000 EGP.

The question is: Is there a negative effect from the debit interest in this company or not?

The answer:

First: Determination of the economic efficiency degree of the product without using debit interest, which is as following:

Determination of Net Profit = Sales Value – (Sales Cost Value + General Expenses Value) =

= 1000 - (600 + 100) = 300

Measuring the economic efficiency degree of the product = (Sales Value - (Sales Cost Value + General Expenses Value) * 0.5) / Net Profit

= (1000 - (600 + 100) * 0.5) / 300 = 2.17

Second: Looking at the previous economic efficiency degree table, we find that a degree of 2.17 is equal to very good.

Third: Determination of the economic efficiency degree of the product by using debit interest, which is as following:

Determination of Net Profit = Sales Value – (Sales Cost Value + General Expenses Value + Debit Interest Value) = 1000 - (600 + 100 + 200) = 100

Measuring the economic efficiency degree of the product = (Sales Value -
(Sales Cost Value + General Expenses Value + Debit Interest Value) * 0.5) /
Net Profit = (1000 - (600 + 100 + 200) * 0.5) / 100 = 5.5

Fourth: Looking at the previous economic efficiency degree table, we find
that a degree of 5.5 is equal to good.

Fifth: Looking at the table for determining the effect of debit interest or not,
we find that there is a negative effect of debit interest, and this is because
the economic efficiency degree of the product without the debit interest,
which was very good degree, it has fallen to a good degree. If there is no
insolvency in its financial liquidity, the company continues to pay off the
loan and its interest, or the financial manager must alert the top
administration of the company to replace the loan and its interest by offering
the alternative, which is to increase the capital.

Here we will use one of the mathematical equations of geometric genetic economy theory as follows:

First: Determination of the economic efficiency degree of product without using credit interest, which is as following:

Determination of Net Profit = Sales Value – (Sales Cost Value + General Expenses Value+ Debit Interest Value, if any) =

Measuring the economic efficiency degree of the product = (Sales Value - (Sales Cost Value + General Expenses Value+ Debit Interest Value, if any) * 0.5) / Net Profit

Second: Determination of the economic efficiency degree of the product by using credit interest, which is as follows:

Determination of Net Profit = (Sales Value + Credit Interest Value) – (Sales Cost Value + General Expenses Value + Debit Interest Value, if any) =

Measuring the economic efficiency degree of the product = ((Sales Value + Credit Interest Value) - (Sales Cost Value + General Expenses Value + Debit Interest Value, if any) * 0.5)) / Net Profit

Third: We compare the economic efficiency degree of the product by using the credit interest with the economic efficiency degree of the product without using the credit interest to find out whether there is a positive effect of the credit interest or not according to the following table:

The following table determines whether there is a positive effect in credit interest or not

In case if the economic efficiency degree of the product without using credit interest is excellent

If the economic efficiency degree of the product by using credit interest became excellent then, there is no positive effect of credit interest

In case if the economic efficiency degree of the product without using credit interest is very good

If the economic efficiency degree of the product by using credit interest became very good then, there is no positive effect of credit interest

Or the economic efficiency degree of the product by using credit interest became – excellent then, there is a positive effect of credit interest

In case if the economic efficiency degree of the product without using credit interest is good

If the economic efficiency degree of the product by using credit interest became good then, there is no positive effect of credit interest

Or the economic efficiency degree of the product by using credit interest became – excellent – very good then, there is a positive effect of credit interest

In case if the economic efficiency degree of the product without using credit interest is acceptable

If the economic efficiency degree of the product by using credit interest became acceptable then, there is no positive effect of credit interest

Or the economic efficiency degree of the product by using credit interest became excellent – very good - good then, there is a positive effect of credit interest

In case if the economic efficiency degree of the product without using credit interest is weak

If the economic efficiency degree of the product by using credit interest became weak then, there is no positive effect of credit interest

Or the economic efficiency degree of the product by using credit interest became excellent – very good - good – acceptable then, there is a positive effect of credit interest

In case if the economic efficiency degree of the product without using credit interest is very weak

If the economic efficiency degree of the product by using credit interest became very weak then, there is no positive effect of credit interest

Or the economic efficiency degree of the product by using credit interest became excellent – very good - good – acceptable – weak then, there is a positive effect of credit interest

In case if the economic efficiency degree of the product without using credit interest is losses

If the economic efficiency degree of the product by using credit interest became losses then, there is no positive effect of credit interest

Or the economic efficiency degree of the product by using credit interest became excellent – very good - good – acceptable – weak – very weak then, there is a positive effect of credit interest

Treating the effect of the credit interest.

If the comparison is made according to the table of determining the effect of the credit interest or not, and it is found that there is a positive effect of the credit interest, thereupon the financial manager should look into the following two possibilities:

The first possibility: Why did the company resort to credit interest and did not use the money of its deposits in its activity? If there was a temporary recession in its activity and it exploited its liquidity in these deposits, then this is good.

The second possibility: As for if the credit interest situation continues, the financial manager should discuss with the top administration and the marketing manager to know why the market did not absorb the excess liquidity in the company's activity and is there a possibility to open a new market that exploits this liquidity or not.

In order to explain this subject for us, we will give this practical example, which is as following:

If you are a financial manager and you have the following data:

The cost value of the product unit is 600 EGP, and the share of the product from the general expenses is 100 EGP, the product's share of the debit interest is 100 EGP, the product's share of the credit interest is 200 EGP, and the sale value of the product unit is 1000 EGP.

The question is: Is there a positive effect of the credit interest in this company or not, and what is the treatment?

The answer:

Here we will use one of the mathematical equations of geometric genetic economy theory as follows:

First: Determination of the economic efficiency degree of product without using credit interest, which is as following:

Determination of Net Profit = Sales Value − (Sales Cost Value + General Expenses Value + Debit Interest Value, if any) = 1000 - (600 + 100 + 100) = 200

Measuring the economic efficiency degree of the product = (Sales Value - (Sales Cost Value + General Expenses Value + Debit Interest Value, if any) * 0.5) / Net Profit = (1000 - (600 + 100 + 100) * 0.5) / 200 = 3

Second: Looking at the previous efficiency degree table, we find that a degree of 3 is equal to very good

Third: Determination of the economic efficiency degree of the product by using credit interest, which is as following:

Determination of Net Profit = (Sales Value + Credit Interest Value) – (Sales Cost Value + General Expenses Value + Debit Interest Value, if any) = (1000 + 200) - (600 + 100 + 100) = 400

Measuring the economic efficiency degree of the product = ((Sales Value + Credit Interest Value) - (Sales Cost Value + General Expenses Value + Debit Interest Value, if any) * 0.5)) / Net Profit

= ((1000 + 200) - (600 + 100 + 100) * 0.5) / 400 = 2

Fourth: Looking at the previous efficiency degree table, we find that a degree of 2 is equal to excellent

Fifth: Looking at the table for determining the effect of credit interest or not, we find that there is a positive effect of credit interest, and this is due to the economic efficiency degree of the product without the credit interest, which was very good, it rose to excellent when we used the credit interest. Here, the financial manager must look at the reasons that led to use of the liquidity in the form of deposits. Is this credit interest a temporary case or is it required to open new markets to exploit financial liquidity?

Summary of this chapter:

Through this chapter, we got to know some of the tasks of the financial manager, which are as following:

Knowing the degree of economic efficiency of the company's products. (By using the elements of the trading account).

Determine the extent of the effect of the general expenses, the debit interest, and the credit interest on the results of the company. (By using elements of profit and loss account).

Knowing the treatment of these effects, if any.

In this chapter: The reader will learn some of the tasks of the financial manager and the general manager as well as the shareholders or the owners of the company as follows:

The reasons for knowing the efficiency degree of the company's employees in managing the basic activity of the company.

What is meant by managing the basic activity of the company?

What is meant by the efficiency degree of the company's employees in managing the basic activity of the company?

What are the reasons that lead to weak the efficiency degree of the company's employees in managing the basic activity of the company?

How do we measure the degree of efficiency of the company's employees in managing the basic activity of the company?

How do we deal with the weak efficiency degree of the company's employees in managing the basic activity of the company?

Why does the company prepare an estimated budget?

Practical example.

The reasons for knowing the efficiency degree of the company's employees in managing the basic activity of the company.

The reasons for knowing the efficiency degree of the company's employees in managing the basic activity of the company

The first reason: It is among the tasks of the financial manager and the general manager to identify the degree of efficiency of the company's employees in managing the basic activity of the company in order to ensure the extent to which the company achieves its goals.

The second reason: As for the shareholders or the owners of the company, they must know the efficiency degree of the company's employees in managing the basic activity of the company in order to know the company's ability to achieve profits that they obtain.

What is meant by managing the basic activity of the company?

Managing the basic activity of the company is to manage the working capital of the company (in terms of preparing the product - either by producing it or buying it - then selling it and collecting its value) in order to achieve the gross profit that must be able to cover all administrative and general expenses, and thus there is net profit must be equivalent to the capital of the company.

What is meant by the efficiency degree of the company's employees in managing the basic activity of the company?

The efficiency of managing the basic activity of the company is the ability of the company's administrators to repeat the number of working capital turnover in one fiscal year in order to maximize the net profits of the company.

What are the reasons that lead to weak the efficiency degree of the company's employees in managing the basic activity of the company?

The reasons that lead to weak of efficiency degree in managing the basic activity of the company are summarized as follows:

Weak of administration efficiency (the human element), whether the production department, marketing department, or follow up the higher administration (this is due to the presence of a defect or deficiency in the systems and regulations followed in the company).

The existence of a material problem that disrupted the working capital turnover (such as equipment, money, raw material).

There is a deficiency in the quality of the product.

here is weak purchasing power for consumers.

Here we will use one of the mathematical equations of geometric genetic economy theory as follows:

Calculating Net Profit = (Sales Value) - (Sales Cost Value + General Expenses Value)

Calculating the efficiency degree of managing the basic activity of the company = (Asset Value) - (Asset Value - Net Profit) * 0.5) / Net Profit

Where the efficiency degrees of managing the basic activity of the company are divided into:

(Excellent - Very Good - Good - Acceptable - Weak - Losses)

How do we deal with the weak efficiency degree of the company's employees in managing the basic activity of the company?

Treatment of weakness in the efficiency degree of managing the basic activity of the company is by avoiding the causes of weakness, which we mentioned previously, which are as following:

With regard to weak of administration efficiency (the human element), whether the production department, marketing department, or follow up the higher administration (this is due to the presence of defect or deficiency in the systems and regulations followed in the company), so the administrators must determine the required tasks for each employee and the required time for each task following the correct systems and regulations in the company.

As for the existence of a material problem that disrupted the working capital turnover (such as equipment, money, raw material), the financial manager must search for the reason for that, and this is due to one of the two reasons, namely:

First reason: there is malfunction occurred (technical or material) in one of the elements of the working capital turnover (in the purchases department - stores department - production department - marketing department - collection management). The financial manager works to treat this malfunction after determining the department in which the malfunction occurred.

Second reason: That there was a deficit in the liquidity of the company that led to a slowdown in the working capital turnover, the financial manager must work to provide this liquidity through facilities, loans, or increasing the capital.

As for the deficiency in the product quality, the financial manager must meet with the higher administration and with each of the production manager, as well as the marketing manager and the manager of the company's research department to know the reasons that led to the weakness of the product quality in order to treat this weakness.

As for the existence of weak purchasing power for consumers and this is known through the Marketing manager as well as through products that compete with the products of the company. The treatment for this is to grant facilities to customers or installments through banks if the product allows this, otherwise, new markets must be opened, whether internal or external which has greater purchasing power.

Why does the company prepare an estimated budget?

Reasons for preparing the company's estimated budget are summarized as follows:

The estimated budget provides an opportunity to compare what has been done with what was planned in the estimated budget to know the deviations and their causes and treat these deviations firstly.

Placing everyone in the company with his responsibilities entrusted to him.

The estimated budget helps in making decisions regarding reward and punishment based on what has been achieved from the estimated budget.

If you are a financial manager, general manager, shareholder of the company or the owner of the company, and you have the following data:

Sales Value = 1000 EGP

Sales Cost Value = 600 EGP

General Expenses Value = 350 EGP

Total Assets Value = 10,000 EGP

The required: calculate the efficiency degree of the employees in managing the basic activity of the company and what is the treatment that you suggest?

The answer:

Here we will use one of the mathematical equations of geometric genetic economy theory as follows:

Calculating Net Profit = (Sales Value) - (Sales Cost Value + General Expenses Value)

= (1000) - (600 + 350) = 50

Calculating the efficiency degree of managing the basic activity of the company = (Asset Value) - (Asset Value - Net Profit) * 0.5) / Net Profit

= ((10000) - (10000 - 50) * 0.5) / 50 = 100.5

By looking at the previous table of efficiency degrees, we find that a degree of 100.5 is equal to very weak, and this indicates a low rate of working capital turnover, and thus the company failed to achieve profits equivalent to the available economic resources, and this is due to one of the following reasons:

Weak of administration efficiency (the human element), whether the production department, marketing department, or follow up the higher administration (this is due to the presence of a defect or deficiency in the followed systems and regulations in the company).

The existence of a material problem that disrupted the working capital turnover (such as equipment, money, raw material).

There is a deficiency in the quality of the product.

The existence of weak in purchasing power for consumers.

For treatment the weakness of efficiency degree of the company's employees in managing the basic activity of the company, it is to avoid the causes of weakness, which we mentioned previously, which are as following:

With regard to weak of administration efficiency which may be due to the human element, as the higher administration didn't follow up the different other departments whether the production department, marketing department (this is due to the presence of defect or deficiency in the followed systems and regulations in the company), so the higher administration must determine the required tasks for each employee in the company and the required time for each task following the correct systems and regulations in the company.

As for the existence of a material problem that disrupted the working capital turnover (such as equipment, money, raw material), the financial manager must search for the reason for that, and this is due to one of the two reasons, namely:

First reason: there is malfunction occurred (technical or material) in one of the elements of the working capital turnover (in the purchases department - stores department - production department - marketing department - collection management). The financial manager works to treat this malfunction after determining the department in which the malfunction occurred.

Second reason: That there was a deficit in the liquidity of the company that led to a slowdown in the working capital turnover, the financial manager must work to provide this liquidity through facilities, loans, or increasing the capital.

As for the deficiency in the product quality, the financial manager must meet with the higher administration and with each of the production manager, as well as the marketing manager and the manager of the company's research department to know the reasons that led to weakness of the product quality in order to treat this weakness.

As for the existence of weak purchasing power for consumers and this is known through the Marketing manager as well as through products that compete with the products of the company. The treatment for this is to grant facilities to customers or installments through banks if the product allows this, otherwise, new markets must be opened, whether internal or external which has greater purchasing power.

After identifying the deficiencies and treating this deficiency, as we mentioned in the previous lines, the company must prepare an estimated budget that the employees of the company are obligated to implement in order to achieve profits equivalent to the available economic resources to this company.

Here we will use one of the mathematical equations of geometric genetic economy theory as follows:

First: Calculating the economic efficiency degree of product.

Why do we calculate the economic efficiency degree of the product of this company? Because it will be used during the preparation of the estimated budget, and the aim is to preserve the type of activity that this company is practicing.

Calculation of Gross Profit = Sales Value - Sales Cost Value = 1000 - 600 = 400

Calculating of the economic efficiency degree of product = (Sales Value - (Sales Cost Value * 0.5))/ Gross profit

= (1000 - (600 * 0.5)) / 400 = 1.75

Second: Determination of the equivalent net profit to the available resources for this company as follows:

The degree of the standard of equivalent net profit to the available resources is = 4.5, with a good degree, which is the beginning of the safety point, and it is used in the case of economic depression.

The degree of the standard of equivalent net profit to the available resources is = 3.5 with a very good degree, and it is used in the case of the beginning of the economic boom.

The degree of the standard of equivalent net profit to the available resources is = 2.5 with a very good degree and it is used in the case of economic recovery.

Therefore, we will use in preparing the estimated budget for this company the standard degree of equivalent net profit, which is equal to 4.5 with a good degree

Calculation of equivalent net profit for available resources

Efficiency degree of the estimated budget = (Total Assets - (Total Assets - Equivalent Net Profit) * 0.5) / Equivalent Net Profit

Assume that the equivalent net profit = B, and therefore the previous equation is as follows:

4.5 = (10,000 - (10,000 - B) * 0.5) / B

4.5B = (10,000 - 5,000 + 0.5B)

4B = 5000

B = 1250

Thus, the equivalent net profit equals 1250

Third: Calculating the gross profit of this company

Gross profit = equivalent net profit + general expenses value

= 1250 + 350 = 1600

Fourth: Calculating the sales value and the sales cost value of the estimated budget of this company.

By using the previous gross profit that equals to 1600 and the economic efficiency degree of the product that was previously achieved, which was equal to 1.75, we can obtain the sales value and sales cost value for this company through the following equations:

Sales Cost Value = ((Gross Profit * the economic efficiency degree of product) - (Gross Profit)) * 2

= ((1600 * 1.75) - (1600)) * 2

= (2800 - 1600) * 2 = 2400

Sales Value = Sales Cost Value + Gross Profit

= 2400 + 1600 = 4000

Fifth: From the above, the estimated budget for this company can be written as follows:

Estimated budget, with a good degree.

Sales Value =	4000
Minus Sales Cost Value =	2,400
Gross Profit =	1600
Minus General Expenses Value =	350
Equivalent net profit =	1250

Sixth: In order to make sure that the estimated budget has been prepared in a proper way, by making sure that the economic efficiency degree of product has not changed, which was equal to 1.75 (meaning that the type of activity of this company did not change when preparing the estimated budget), we make sure of this through the following equations:

Calculation of gross profit of the estimated budget = Sales Value - Sales Cost Value = 4000 - 2400 = 1600

Calculation of the economic efficiency degree of product of the estimated budget = (Sales Value - (Sales Cost Value * 0.5))/ Gross Profit

$$= (4000 - (2400 * 0.5)) / 1600 = 1.75$$

Note:

One of the scientific miracles of the genetic economy is that it determined the type of economic activity of this company (by means of the economic efficiency degree of the product (which is one of the mathematical equations of geometric genetic economy theory), which was 1.75, which was re-used in preparing the estimated budget in order to preserve the type of activity of this company. If we assume that this activity of the company is real estate activity at the economic efficiency degree of product 1.75. When evaluating the estimated budget, we find that the economic efficiency degree of product is the same as 1.75

Another example:

If you are a financial manager, general manager, the shareholder of the company or the owner of the company, and you have been presented with the following data:

The sale price of the product per unit = 10 EGP

The cost value of the product per unit = 8 EGP

The annual value of general expenses = 250000 EGP

Total asset value = 1500000 EGP

The degree of the equivalent net profit from the available resources is = 4.5, with a good degree, which is the beginning of the safety point, and it is used in the case of economic depression.

The required: Prepare the estimated budget only and make sure of its correctness.

We leave the solution of this example for the generous reader.

Summary of this chapter:

Through this chapter, we got to know one of the most important tasks of the financial manager and the general manager, as well as the task of the owners of property rights or the owners of the company to know the efficiency degree of their company in terms of:

Knowing the reasons that lead to the weak degree of efficiency of managing the basic activity of the company and how to treat these reasons.

How to measure the efficiency degree of managing the basic activity of the company.

Using the estimated budget to improve the company's results.

The principles to be used concerning bank credit.

In this chapter: The reader will learn some of the tasks of the bank credit employee, the financial manager, the general manager, and the owners of the company as follows:

What is meant by bank credit?

Elements of the bank credit.

Knowing the company's ability to repay the loan and its interest by using financial analysis.

The criticisms directed to financial analysis.

Knowing the company's ability to repay the loan and its interest by using the basic estimated budget and the credit budget.

Advantages of using the basic budget and credit budget in granting credit to companies.

Practical example.

What is meant by bank credit: It is one of the activities carried out by banks. As these banks lend to others (whether individuals or companies) for obtaining return with a certain percentage of the value of the loan.

Elements of bank credit

The following conditions must be met in bank credit:

Name of Lender (Bank).

Name of the borrower (individual or company).

The loan amounts.

The date of borrowing.

The interest rate on the loan.

Method, dates, and value of repayment of this loan.

The guarantees required for granting this loan and the conditions for these guarantees.

In this chapter, we will talk about bank credit from the point of view of the lender (the bank) and from the point of view of the borrower (the company)

First: From the point of view of the lender (the bank).

We know that the bank lends to both individuals, companies, and others. But in this chapter, we will restrict ourselves to lending to companies only, which is the field of specialization of this book.

When the bank credit employee deals with a company wishing to obtain credit, he interests in two elements, after making all inquiries about this company, namely:

First element: getting all the guarantees related to this loan.

Second element: identification of the company's ability to repay the loan and its interest.

Here a very important question appears: How does the bank credit employee know the company's ability to pay off the loan and its interest?

The answer is that among the many requests that is required to be fulfilled by the company, the bank credit employee requests three approved balance sheets so the bank credit employee can analysis these balance sheets by using financial analysis tools in order to know the company's ability to repay the loan and its interest.

Where the financial ratios are divided into four main sections, which are:

Liquidity ratios.

Profitability ratios.

Efficiency ratios.

Financial leverage ratios.

The following is an explanation of those ratios.

First: Liquidity Ratios

They are the ratios that measure the extent of the firm's ability to meet its short-term liabilities when due by using its liquid and semi-liquid assets (current assets) without achieving losses.

Current Ratio

Current Ratio = Current Assets / Current Liabilities

This ratio expresses the number of times that current assets can cover current liabilities, and the higher this ratio indicates the company's ability to face the risks of the sudden settlement of current liabilities without the need to liquidate any fixed assets or obtain new borrowing.

However, we go back to point out that this ratio cannot be deafly read, so the increase in the ratio is a good thing, but the increase can be acceptable to a certain degree. The cash item may be exaggerated, which indicates that the company does not use its liquidity well and reduces profitability as a result, or perhaps due to the increase in the accumulation of the customers' item and inflated as a result of not using good policies in the collection and follow-up of debtor customers.

Therefore, the ratio should be read and compared as we indicated with the average ratios achieved for successful companies in the same activity, as well as taking into account all other aspects that can be deduced from the ratio and its relationship to other items.

Quick Ratio

Cash Ratio = (Current Assets - Inventory) / Current Liabilities

This the ratio shows the extent of the possibility of paying short-term liabilities within a few days. The inventory item is avoided as it is one of the least liquid elements of current assets and also because it is difficult to dispose of it within a short time without achieving losses.

The cash Ratio

Cash ratio = cash and semi cash assets / current liabilities

This ratio shows the extent to which short-term liabilities can be repaid and gives an indication to management that during the bad times, short-term liabilities can be repaid.

The semi-monetary assets are all that can be converted into cash within a short period, such as negotiable securities on the stock exchange. Here, this question arises: Does the payment with semi-monetary assets affect the working capital turnover or not?

Second: Profitability ratios.

They are the ratios that measure the efficiency of management in optimally utilizing the resources to achieve profits.

Gross Profit Margin.

Gross profit margin = gross profit / net sales

This ratio shows the relationship between net sales revenue and the cost of goods sold, and this ratio must be compared with the average ratios achieved in this sector, as the decrease in the ratio may reflect an exaggerated increase in the cost of raw materials used in production or indirect labor cost or otherwise.

Rate of Return on Sales (Net Profit Margin)

Net Profit Margin = Net Profit / Net Sales

This ratio measures the net profit achieved on each dollar of sales, and it refers to the percentage of profits achieved by sales after covering the cost of sales and all other expenses, including administrative and general expenses, financing expenses, etc.

The higher this ratio, this is better. This ratio must be compared with the average ratios achieved in this sector. Also, this ratio should not be used alone. Perhaps, despite the high ratio in many cases, the company does not achieve an appropriate rate of return on equity.

Return on Equity

Rate of return on equity = Net Profit / Equity

This ratio expresses the return that the owners achieve on investing their money in the company, and it is considered one of the most important profitability ratios used since, based on this ratio, the owners may decide to continue the activity, or transfer the funds to other investments that achieve an appropriate return.

Third: Efficiency / Activity ratios:

They are financial ratios that evaluate how efficiently of the company by using the assets and liabilities to achieve sales and maximum profits. Asset turnover ratio, inventory turnover and days in inventory sales are the basic efficiency ratios.

Fourth: Leverage Ratios

They are the ratios that measure the extent of the company's dependence on financing on external sources.

Total assets to liabilities.

Total assets to liabilities = Total assets /Total liabilities

This ratio shows the extent to which total liabilities can be covered by using total assets and the higher this ratio, which is better from the viewpoint of external investors and lenders.

Total equity to liabilities ratio

Total equity to liabilities = Total equity/ Total liabilities

This ratio indicates the extent to which total liabilities can be covered by using total equity.

Interest Coverage Ratio

Interest Coverage Ratio = Net Profit Before Interest and Tax / Interest Expense

This ratio shows the ability to cover the debit interest of the loans and bonds using the net operating profit. The higher this ratio, this is better for the company.

Net Working Capital to Long-term Debt

Working Capital to Long Term Loans = Working Capital /Long-term Debt

This ratio shows how long-term loans can be covered by using working capital.

Financial ratios use the relationship of a certain element to another element (numerator and denominator) and therefore the person who do the analysis is the one who determines the relationship of these two elements to each other, as he can manipulate this relationship to extract the specific result he wants.

By reviewing all the previous financial ratios, we find that the ratios use the basic elements of the company's balance sheet to extract the company's ability to use these elements in paying its liabilities, including the bank's loan. As the bank asks the company's administrators to liquidate the company by using those elements (whether the current assets that are used in the working capital turnover or the fixed assets that the company's activity cannot dispense with) which is the basis of the company's business for fulfillment of the loan repayment.

When the company's administrators decided to borrow from the bank, did they think in case the insolvent, they will liquidate the company, or did they want to develop the company's business and improve its results?

Here, a very important question appears what is the lending approach that the bank must follow when lending to companies in order to make sure of the company's ability to repay the loan and its interest?

The answer is summarized as follows:

Preparing an estimated budget (part of estimated budget profits can be cut to pay one of the loan installments).

Preparing a credit budget (to pay the annual debit interest).

If the company can achieve these budgets, this places the company in front of its responsibility in achieving these budgets in front of the bank.

If the company is not able to achieve these budgets, this avoids the company being difficult to repay the loan and its interest.

Through the net profits of the basic budget, the company can pay one of the loans installments.

The company will pay the debit interest on the loan through the credit budget.

In this approach, there is no pressure on the balance sheet elements resulting from its use to repay the loan, and hence the company is not exposed to liquidation

In this approach, the banks have reduced the risk rate due to the reduction in business insolvency.

By using the budgets approach, the banks contribute to eliminate the economic depression, and this is due to:

The banks play the role of the state in providing funds for increasing the production of companies (an alternative to government spending policy to treat the economic depression that is established by the economist Keynes).

In case the wheel of production is activated in the state, this leads to increase in purchasing power.

When the banks reduce the loan interest, they contribute to success of the companies, which eliminates unemployment.

Practical example.

If you are a credit employee at a bank, and you are offered the latest balance sheet for a company that wants to borrow half a million dollars at an annual interest rate of 10%, and these balance sheet data are as following:

Sales Value = 1100000 $

Sales Cost Value = 800000 $

Total General Expenses Value = 250000 $

Total fixed and current assets = 1500000 $

The standard degree of the basic estimated budget is = 4.5, with a good degree, which is the beginning of the safety point, and it is used in the case of economic depression.

The required:

Preparing the company's basic estimated budget.

Preparing the credit budget to cover the debit interest of the loan.

The answer:

Preparing the company's basic estimated budget.

Calculation of loan interest = loan amount * annual loan interest rate

Calculation of loan interest = 500000 * 10% = 50000 $

Calculation of the total resources to the company =

(Total assets + total loan amount)

1500000 + 500000 = 2000000 $

Now, we can prepare the company's basic estimated budget with a good degree, according to the following steps.

Here, we will use one of the mathematical equations of geometric genetic economy theory as follows:

First: Calculation of the economic efficiency degree of product

Calculation of Gross Profit = Sales Value – Sales Cost Value = 1100000 - 800000 = 300000

Calculation of the economic efficiency degree of product = (Sales Value - (Sales Cost Value * 0.5)) / Gross Profit

= (1100000 - (800000 * 0.5)) / 300000 = 2.333333

Second: Determination of the equivalent net profit.

The standard degree of the basic estimated budget = (Total Assets - (Total Assets - Equivalent Net Profit) * 0.5) / Equivalent Net Profit

Assume that the equivalent net profit = B, and therefore the previous equation is as follows:

4.5 = (2000000 - (2000000 - B) * 0.5) / B

4.5B = (2000000 - 1000000 + 0.5B)

4B = 1000000

B = 250000

Thus, the equivalent net profit equals 250000

Third: Calculation of the gross profit of this company

Gross profit = equivalent net profit + general expenses value = 250000 + 250000 = 500000

Fourth: Calculation of the sales value and the sales cost value of the estimated budget of this company.

We will use the previous gross profit, which equals 500000 and the economic efficiency degree of product, which was equal to 2.333333

The following equations can be used to obtain the sales value and sales cost value for this company:

Sales Cost Value = ((Gross Profit * the economic efficiency degree of product) - (Gross Profit)) * 2

= ((500000 * 2.333333) - (500000)) * 2

= (1166666.5 - 500000) * 2 = 1333333

Sales Value = Sales Cost Value + Gross Profit Value

= 1333333 + 500000 = 1833333

From the above, the basic estimated budget for this company can be written as follows:

Basic estimated budget with a good degree.

Sales Value =	1833333
Minus the Sales Cost Value =	1333333
Gross profit =	500000
Minus General Expenses Value =	250000
Equivalent net profit =	250000

In order to make sure that the estimated budget has been prepared in a proper manner, by making sure that the economic efficiency degree of the product has not changed, which was equal to 2.333333 (meaning that the type of activity of this company did not change when we prepared the estimated budget), we will make sure of this through the following equations:

Calculation OF Gross Profit = Sales Value - Sales Cost Value = 1833333 - 1333333 = 500,000

Calculating the economic efficiency degree of product = (Sales value - (Sales cost value * 0.5))/ Gross profit = (1833333 - (1333333 * 0.5)) / 500000 = 2.333333

We will use the value of the cost of credit, which is equal to 50000 $ (which must be equal to the gross profit of the credit budget because the gross profit is required to cover the cost of credit) and the economic efficiency degree of product that was previously achieved, which was equal to 2.333333

The following equation can be used to obtain the sales value and sales cost value for this company:

Sales Cost Value = ((Gross Profit * the economic efficiency degree of product) - (Gross Profit)) * 2

= ((50000 * 2.333333) - (50000)) * 2

= (116666.65-50000) * 2 = 133333.3

Sales Value = Sales Cost Value + Gross Profit Value

= 133333.3+ 50000 = 183333.3

From the above, we can prepare the credit budget for this company as follows:

Credit budget with a good grade

Value of Excess Sales =	183333.3
Minus the Sales Cost Value=	133333.3
Gross Profit =	50000
Minus debit interest =	50000
Net profit =	0.00

The company must achieve the basic estimated budget and the credit budget together as follows:

The sales value of the basic estimated budget = 1833333

Add the value of excess sales to cover debit interest = 183333.3

Total annual sales value to be achieved by marketing manager = 2016666.3

Here the bank credit employee asks the company administrator if the company's marketing manager can market the value of the total annual sales (2016666.3). If the answer is:

Yes, then the bank deals with this company on this loan.

No, then the bank does not deal with this company on this loan.

When the company needs funds, it must use the estimated budget approach to find out the company's ability to repay the loan and its interest.

If the company can repay the loan and its interest, it is preferable to use the loan to increase the production process.

If the company is unable to repay the loan and its interest, it is preferable that the company uses the alternative, which is to increase the capital so that it does not enter into problems that may lead to liquidation.

Another practical example: The solution to this question is left to the reader.

If you are a financial manager and the higher administration asked you to study the company's desire to borrow an amount of one million pounds at an annual interest of 10%, and the available data to you were as following:

The unit selling price = 10 EGP

Unit cost = 8 EGP

Total general expenses = 200000 EGP

Total fixed and current assets (the available resources to the company) = 1000000 EGP

The standard degree of the basic estimated budget is = 4.5, with a good degree, which is the beginning of the safety point, and it is used in the case of economic depression.

The required:

Preparing the company's basic estimated budget.

Preparing the credit budget to cover the debit interest of the loan.

Your decision, which you will present to the higher administration.

Summary of this chapter:

Through this chapter, we got to know one of the most important tasks of the credit employee in the bank, as well as the task of the financial manager and general manager that are working in the company which wishes to deal with bank credit, as well as how the owners of property rights or the owners of the company made the decision to borrow from banks in terms of:

Knowing the alternative approach (approach to preparing the basic estimated budget and preparing the credit budget instead of using the financial ratios approach in financial analysis), which guarantees the success of the credit process for both the bank that grants the loan and the company which takes this loan.

In this chapter: The reader will learn some of the tasks of the financial manager, the general manager, and the economic consultants as follows:

The types of influences that affect the company's activity.

The extent of the impact of those influences (positively or negatively) on the company's activity.

Identification of the four elements that affect the working capital turnover rate.

Determination of the economic elements related to the economic situation that the country is going through and their impact on the company's activity.

The principles to be considered when the sales cost value increases for the company to continue competing in the market.

The principles to be considered when the company gives discounts on the selling price for the company to continue competing in the market.

Practical examples.

Introduction:

All companies do not operate in isolation from the environment in which they operate. They affect and are affected by the environment, whether these influences are negative or positive, which compel the companies to adapt to these variables in order to continue in the working market by taking the appropriate decision to face these variables.

Types of influences:

Legal influences (when the law regulates a specific activity).

Natural and social influences (such as natural disasters – the emergence of diseases such as the Coronavirus).

Political influences (such as wars).

Economic influences (such as recession - unemployment ... etc.)

Here this question appears: from where do we know about these influences that affected the company activity, whether positively or negatively?

The answer is:

We know these influences through the rate of working capital turnover. In the third chapter, we discussed determination of the efficiency degree of the company's employees in managing the basic activity of the company and we discussed the following:

If the working capital turnover rate achieves profits equivalent to the available resources to the company, we conclude that there are positive influences that achieved these profits

If the working capital turnover rate does not achieve profits equivalent to the available resources to the company, we conclude that there are negative influences that affected the achievement of profits.

The question:

What are the influences that affect the rate of working capital turnover (starting from purchasing of raw materials - manufacturing and production - marketing - selling and collection of sales values)?

The answer:

The influences that affect the rate of working capital turnover are summarized in four elements as follows:

The first element: Weak of administration efficiency (the human element), whether the production department, marketing department, or follow up the higher administration (this is due to the presence of a defect or deficiency in the followed systems and regulations in the company).

The second element: The existence of a material problem that disrupted the working capital turnover (such as equipment, money, raw material).

The third element: There is a deficiency in the quality of the product.

The fourth element: The existence of weak purchasing power for consumers.

Regarding the first element, which is weak of efficiency of the human element, we discussed in the first chapter how the human resource manager chooses the members of the different departments (production - marketing - financial - the general manager) and how he puts the right man in the right job. As well as the administrators must implement and follow the systems and regulations in the company.

Regarding the second element, which is the existence of a material problem that disrupted the working capital turnover, we discussed this problem as follows:

In the second chapter of this book, we discussed how the financial manager manages the company's finances and identifies their effect on the result of the activity by determination of the extent of the impact of general expenses, debit interest, and credit interest on the company's results.

In the fourth chapter, we discussed the company's need for liquidity through the extent of the company's validity in dealing with bank credit. If the company was able to implement the basic estimated budget and the credit budget, it deals with bank credit to provide the liquidity that it needs, otherwise the company seeks to increase its capital.

Regarding the third element, there is the deficiency in product quality. This deficiency must be known through the company, because the company is the most knowledgeable one of the techniques of its product, and on another hand, the technical field of product manufacture is outside the approach that is presented by this book.

Regarding the fourth element, which is the presence of low purchasing power for consumers; this is what we will explain through the following economic elements.

Here, we will summarize the economic elements that are related to the economic situation of the State and they have impact on the company's activity through these questions:

Is the company's product an essential product or a luxury product?

How often per year do the company's customers need these products?

What is the value of the product versus the income of the company's clients in the year?

What is the state of purchasing power of the company's customers?

Are the company's customers in the local market or in foreign markets (the case of exportation)?

Does the state support the company's product or not?

Is installment system appropriate for companies' products or not?

Are there local or foreign market competitors (in case of importation) for the product?

In the following lines, we will answer these above questions to find out the significance of each question and its impact on the purchasing power of the company's customers.

The answer of the first question: Is the company's product an essential product or a luxury product? Here, the company must determine whether its product is a necessary product or a luxury product, because in a state of depression, which weakens the purchasing power, people try to keep their money and only spend it on necessary product, as necessary product has priority in spending, so the owners of luxury products must find solutions to encourage their customers to buy their products through the following (the presence of installment systems for the product proportional to the purchasing power of their customers - Reducing the prices of their products in the case that these products allow this, as we will explain in the following) or finding new customers with greater purchasing power, whether in the local or foreign markets).

The answer of the second question: How many times in the year the company's customers need these products? The products differ from each other in the extent to which customers need the companies' products. For example, the customer's need for food is daily, as for clothes, it is seasonal. As for cars, it depends on the desire of car customers for buying. What is the importance of knowing the number of times the company's customers need the products of the company in a year? It is for knowing the number of working capital turnover for the company and the suitability of this number to achieve profits that are equivalent to the available resources, after the company knows the available marketing gap, and the company's share in this marketing gap, in the existence of the weak purchasing power of its customers.

The answer of the third question: What is the value of the product in relation to the income of the company's customers in the year? Here we are necessary to know the customer's share value of the company's products and what he consumes during the year. Why? If the ratio of the value of the products that the customer consumes in relation to his annual income is few, the company guarantees the repetition of the working capital turnover. Or the company should increase its advertising to motivate them to buy.

The answer of the fourth question: What is the state of purchasing power of the company's customers? The answer of this question does not depend on the state of recession only, but on the various economic conditions. Why? Because the sales policy and pricing differ according to the state of purchasing power of the company's customers as we will explain at the following:

If the state of purchasing power is strong and differs between classes of society. Here we must apply the Marshall surplus (meaning that the prices of the product start high, as it is directed to the class with large purchasing power, and after a period a discount is made on the selling prices of the product in order to sell it to a segment with less purchasing power and so on).

If the state of purchasing power is weak. Here, the companies need means to motivate these customers through advertising means - installments - reducing of product prices.

The answer of the fifth question: Are the customers of the company in the local market or in the foreign market (The case of exportation)? It is known that there is difference in the standard of living between countries with each other and there is also difference in the exchange rate of the currencies exchanged between countries, so the company must study these markets to choose the market that is appropriate for its products as well as the purchasing power that achieves the profits that the company wants.

The answer of the sixth question: Does the state support the company's product or not? Sometimes some countries provide support with the aim of strengthening the purchasing power by reducing customs on imported materials that enter into the company's production or providing support through the selling price of the product, especially for the necessary products, which allows these companies to continue in the working market.

The answer of the seventh question: Is it valid for the company to deal in installments with its products or not? There are some products that are suitable for installments, such as real estate companies because the number of working capital turnover is by its nature slow, it may sometimes take more than one year and the value of real estate is large, so these companies resort to use the installment system, either through the company or banks, but there are some companies that need to liquidity through collection of the value of their sales to enter it again in many rounds of working capital turnover, such as biscuit companies, and thus the installment period is simple. It may be for a few days, because the biscuit company needs a present purchasing power.

The answer of the eighth question: Are there local or foreign market competitors (in the case of importation) for the product. In case that there are competitors for the company's product, this situation puts the company under pressure to grant an advantage in attracting the purchasing power of customers by granting discounts on selling prices, on the other hand, the pressure continues at the company when the costs of the product increase, where the question becomes: is it possible to sell this product whose costs have increased at its old price, or the company is forced to raise its prices to avoid loss and it loses its competition in the market.

Note: We will discuss later the principles that the company must take into account when it gives discounts on the selling price or when the costs of the product increase in order to continue its competition in the market.

By answering the previous eight questions, we have explained the complete map to any company to deal with purchasing power. Please choose what suits your company from this map.

The aim of the preparing of the budget model when the cost of sales increases.

The company will know the flexibility of the product to absorb the increased costs in order to remain competitive in the markets without the company having to raise prices while achieving the same profits that the company was achieving before the cost rise.

Budget preparing inputs when the cost of sales increases.

The selling price of the unit (product).

Unit cost (product) before cost increase.

Unit cost (product) after the cost increase.

Total annual general expenses.

Total fixed and current assets.

Practical example

In the following we explain how to prepare the budget when the cost of sales increases if we have the following data:

The unit selling price = 10 $

The unit cost before the increase = 8 $

The unit cost after the increase = 9 $

Total general expenses = 250000$

Total Fixed and Current Assets = 1,500,000 $

Preparing the estimated budget when the target budget efficiency with a degree of (4.5) good - the beginning of the safety point

The required:

So, what is your decision when the cost of sales increased for this company?

The answer:

In this case, the following must be prepared:

Preparing the estimated budget with a good degree before the cost increases.

Preparing the estimated budget with a good degree after the cost increases.

Then the company will know the value of the excess sales to be marketed until to achieve the same previous profits.

Here we will use some of the geometric genetic economy theory equations as follows:

First: Determination of the economic efficiency degree of the company's product

Calculation of Gross Profit = Unit Sales Price - Unit Cost = 10 - 8 = 2

Calculation of the economic efficiency degree of product = (Unit Sales Price - (Unit Cost * 0.5)) / Gross Profit = (10 - (8 * 0.5)) / 2 = 3

Second: Determination of the equivalent net profit to the available resources for this company

The estimated budget efficiency degree = (Total assets - (Total assets - Equivalent net profit) * 0.5) / Equivalent net profit

Assume that the equivalent net profit = B, and therefore the previous equation is as following:

4.5 = (1500000 - (1500000 - B) * 0.5) / B

4.5B = (1500000 - 750000 + 0.5B)

4B = 750000

B = 187500

So equivalent net profit equals 187500

Third: Calculation of the gross profit of this company.

Gross profit of the budget = equivalent net profit + value of general expenses = 187500 + 250000

= 437500

Fourth: Calculation of the sales value and the sales cost value of the estimated budget of this company as follows:

We will use the previous gross profit of the budget, which equals 437500 and the previously achieved the economic efficiency degree of product, which was equal to 3, the following equation can be used to obtain the sales value and sales cost value for this company as follows:

Sales Cost Value = ((Gross Profit * the economic efficiency degree of product) - (Gross Profit)) * 2

= ((437500 * 3) - (437500)) * 2

= (1312500 - 437500) * 2 = 1750000

Sales Value = Sales Cost Value + Gross Profit

= 1750000 + 437500 = 2187500

From the above, we can prepare the estimated budget for this company as follows:

Estimated budget before the cost increases, with a good degree.

Sales value =	2187,500
Minus the sales cost value =	1750000
Gross profit =	437500
Minus general expenses =	250000
Equivalent net profit =	187500

Preparing the estimated budget with a good degree after the cost increases

First: Calculation of the economic efficiency degree of product for this company after the cost has increased.

Calculation of gross profit = Unit Sales Price - Unit Sales Cost Value after it has increased = 10 - 9 = 1

Calculation of the economic efficiency degree of the product after cost raised = (Unit Sales Price - (Unit Cost * 0.5)) / Gross Profit = (10 - (9 * 0.5)) / 1 = 5.5

Second: Determination of the equivalent net profit to the available resources for this company.

The estimated budget efficiency degree = (Total Assets - (Total Assets - Equivalent Net Profit.)) * 0.5) / Equivalent Net Profit

Assume that the equivalent net profit = B, and therefore the previous equation is as follows:

4.5 = (1500000 - (1500000 - B) * 0.5) / B

4.5B= (1500000 - 750000 + 0.5B)

4B = 750000

B = 187500

So equivalent net profit equals 187,500

Third: Calculation of the gross profit of this company

Gross profit = equivalent net profit + general expenses value = 187500 + 250000 = 437500

Fourth: Calculation of the sales value and the sales cost value of the estimated budget of this company.

We will use the previous gross profit of the second budget, which equals 437500 and the previously achieved the economic efficiency degree of product, which was equal to 5.5, the following equation can be used to obtain the sales value and sales cost value for this company as follows:

Sales Cost Value = ((Gross Profit * the economic efficiency degree of product) - (Gross Profit)) * 2

= ((437500 * 5.5) - (437500)) * 2

= (2406250 - 437500) * 2 = 3937500

Sales Value = Sales Cost Value+ Gross Profit Value

= 3937500 + 437500 = 4375000

From the above, we can prepare the estimated budget for this company as follows:

Estimated budget after the cost increasing with a good degree.

Sales Value =	4375000
Minus the sales cost value =	3937500
Gross profit =	437500
Minus general expenses =	250000
Net profit =	187500

The sales value increases due to the increase in selling cost.

The sales value after cost increase =4375000

(-) Sales value before cost increase =2187500

Increase in sales value due to increase in cost = 2187500

The basis for making the decision

In the case that the marketing manager is able to sell the sales value after cost increase (43750000), to achieve the same profits that the company was achieving before the cost rise, then the administration adopts this increase without increasing the selling price in order to continue its competition in the market.

The aim of the preparing budget model when granting discounts on the selling price of the product as follows:

The company will know the flexibility of the product to absorb the decrease of selling price in order to remain competitive in the markets without the company having to back down from granting these discounts.

The inputs to prepare the estimated budget for granting discounts on the selling price of the product.

The selling price of the unit (product) before the discount.

The selling price of the unit (product) after the discount.

Unit cost (product).

Total value of annual general expenses.

Total value of fixed and current assets.

Practical example

In the following we explain how to prepare the budget when granting discounts on the selling price of the product if we have the following data:

The unit sale price before the discount = 10$

The unit sale price after the discount = 9 $

Unit cost = 8 $

Total value of general expenses = 250000$

Total value of fixed and current assets = 1,500,000 $

Preparing the estimated budget when the target budget efficiency with a degree of (4.5) good - the beginning of the safety point

The required:

So, what is your decision when granting discounts on the selling price of the product?

The answer:

In this case, the following must be prepared:

Preparing the estimated budget with a good degree before granting discounts on the selling price of the product.

Preparing the estimated budget with a good degree after granting discounts on the selling price of the product.

Then the company will know the value of the excess sales to be marketed until achieving the same previous profits.

Here we will use some of the geometric genetic economy theory equations as follows:

First: Calculation of the economic efficiency degree of product for this company

Calculation of Gross Profit = Unit Sales Price - Unit Cost = 10 - 8 = 2

Calculation of the economic efficiency degree of product = (Unit Sales Price - (Unit Cost * 0.5)) / Gross Profit = (10 - (8 * 0.5)) / 2 = 3

Second: Determination of the equivalent net profit to the available resources for this company

The estimated budget efficiency degree = (Total Assets - (Total Assets - Equivalent Net Profit) * 0.5) / Equivalent Net Profit

Assume that the equivalent net profit = B, and therefore the previous equation is as follows:

4.5 = (1500000 - (1500000 - B) * 0.5) / B

4.5B = (1500000 - 750000 + 0.5B)

4B = 750,000

B = 187500

So equivalent net profit equals 187500

Third: Calculation of the gross profit of budget

Gross profit = equivalent net profit + general expenses value = 187500 + 250000 = 437500

Fourth: Calculation of the sales value and the sales cost value of the estimated budget of this company

We will use the previous gross profit, which equals 437500 and the previously achieved the economic efficiency degree of the product, which was equal to 3, the following equation can obtain the sales value and sales cost value for this company as follows:

Sales Cost Value = ((Gross Profit * the economic efficiency degree of product) - (Gross Profit)) * 2

= ((437500 * 3) - (437500)) * 2

= (1312500 - 437500) * 2 = 1750000

Sales Value = Sales Cost Value + Gross Profit

= 1750000 + 437500 = 2187500

From the above, the estimated budget for this company can be written as follows

Estimated budget with a good degree before calculating the discount on the sale price

Sales value =	2187500
Minus the sales cost value =	1750000
Gross profit =	437500
Minus general expenses =	250000
Equivalent net profit =	187500

Preparing the estimated budget at a good degree after granting the discount.

First: Calculation of the economic efficiency degree of product for this company after granting the discount.

Calculation of Gross Profit = Sales Price Unit - Unit Cost = 9 - 8 = 1

Calculation of the economic efficiency degree of product= (Unit Sales Price - (Unit Cost * 0.5)) / Gross Profit = (9 - (8 * 0.5)) / 1 = 5

Second: Determination of the equivalent net profit to the available resources for this company

The estimated budget efficiency degree = (Total Assets - (Total Assets - Equivalent Net Profit) * 0.5) / Equivalent Net Profit

Assume that the equivalent net profit = B, and therefore the previous equation is as follows:

4.5 = (1500000 - (1500000 - B) * 0.5) / B

4.5B = (1500000 - 750000 + 0.5B)

4B = 750,000

B = 187500

So equivalent net profit equals 187500

Third: Calculation of the gross profit of the budget.

Gross profit = equivalent net profit + general expenses value = 187500 + 250000 = 437500

Fourth: Calculation of the sales value and the sales cost value of the estimated budget of this company

We will use the previous gross profit, which equals 437500 and the previously achieved and the economic efficiency degree of the product, which was equal to 5 the following equation can obtain the sales value and sales cost value for this company:

Sales Cost Value = ((Gross Profit * the economic efficiency degree of product) - (Gross Profit)) * 2

= ((437500 * 5) - (437500)) * 2

= (2187500 - 437500) * 2 = 3500000

Sales Value = Sales Cost Value+ Gross Profit

= 3500000 + 437500 = 3937500

From the above, the estimated budget for this company can be written as follows:

Estimated budget with a good degree after granting the discount on the sale price

Sales value =	3937500
Minus the sales cost value =	3500000
Gross profit =	437500
Minus general expenses =	250000
Equivalent net profit =	187500

The increase in the sales value as a result of granting the discount.

The sales value after granting discount = 3937500

Minus the sales value before granting discount = 2187500

Increase in sales value as a result of granting discounts = 1750000

The basis for making the decision.

In the case that the marketing manager is able to sell the sales value after granting the discount (3937500) to achieve the same profits that the company was achieving before granting the discount, then the administration will approve this discount in order to continue its competition in the market, otherwise the granting of this discount will be reconsidered so that the company does not achieve losses.

Summary of this chapter:

Through this chapter, we got to know one of the most important tasks of the financial manager, the general manager, the marketing manager, as well as the economic consultant in terms of:

Identification of the types of influences that affect the results of the company's activity.

Knowing the impact of these influences on the working capital turnover.

Knowing the map of dealing with the purchasing power that is available in front of the company.

Knowing the basis's that must be met when economic conditions change and affect the company's competition in the market, especially when the cost of the product increases or the company needs to give discounts on the selling price in order to remain in its market.

www.ingramcontent.com/pod-product-compliance
Lightning Source LLC
Chambersburg PA
CBHW060110260726
48658CB00004B/1495